Withdrawn

Fact Finders®

DIARY OF
SALLIE HESTER
A
COVERED WAGON GIRL

by Sallie Hester

CAPSTONE PRESS
a capstone imprint

Fact Finders Books are published by Capstone Press,
1710 Roe Crest Drive, North Mankato, Minnesota 56003
www.capstonepub.com

Library of Congress Cataloging-in-Publication Data
Hester, Sallie.
Diary of Sallie Hester : a covered wagon girl / by Sallie Hester.
pages cm.—(Fact finders. First-person histories)
Summary: "Presents excerpts from the diary of Sallie Hester, a teenager who traveled West on
the Oregon Trail in a wagon train in the mid-1800s"—Provided by publisher.
Includes bibliographical references and index.
ISBN 978-1-4765-4193-8 (library binding)
ISBN 978-1-4765-5136-4 (paperback)
ISBN 978-1-4765-5985-8 (eBook PDF)
1. Hester, Sallie—Diaries—Juvenile literature. 2. Pioneer children—West (U.S.)—Diaries—
Juvenile literature. 3. Girls—West (U.S.)—Diaries—Juvenile literature. 4. Overland journeys to
the Pacific—Juvenile literature. 5. Frontier and pioneer life—West (U.S.)—Juvenile literature.
6. West (U.S.)—Description and travel—Juvenile literature. I. Title.
F593.H47 2014
978'.02—dc23   2013026800

Editorial Credits

Carrie Braulick Sheely, editor; Bobbie Nuytten, designer; Wanda Winch, media researcher;
Laura Manthe, production specialist

Photo Credits

The Bancroft Library: U. of California Berkeley, 13 (right); The Bridgeman Art Library: Peter
Newark Historical Pictures/Private Collection, 7; Capstone, 5; Courtesy of Jen Schulten, cover,
1 (girl); Courtesy of Randall A. Wagner, 19; Gino Dante Borges, www.thewildself.com, www.
animateedu.com, 21; North Wind Picture Archives, 17, 25, 27; Scotts Bluff National Monument:
William Henry Jackson, 29 (top); Shutterstock: Andrzej Sowa, cover (papers), Cameron Cross
(wagon), Cupi, 10, Jeffrey M. Frank, 16, 29 (bottom), Kruglov_Orda, 20, Melinda Fawver, 26,
Picsfive, (paper), Russell Shivley, 22 (bot), Seregam, 24, Stocksnapper, 9, Tom Grundy, 23, Zack
Frank, 12-13; SuperStock: Huntington Library, 15, SuperStock, 4; Wikipedia: Malepheasant (Tim
Kiser), 8; www.printroom.com, 11

Printed in the United States of America in Stevens Point, Wisconsin.
122014   008671R

TABLE OF CONTENTS

A Dangerous Journey West

On March 20, 1849, Sallie Hester began a dangerous journey that changed her life. The 14-year-old girl left Indiana with her family to move to the California Territory.

Between 1841 and 1866, more than 350,000 pioneers made the journey from the eastern United States to western territories such as Oregon and California. These pioneers believed life would be better out West. The overcrowding of the eastern United States had led to unhealthy and uncomfortable living conditions. Disease outbreaks were common in the East, causing many deaths.

Pioneers also traveled west in search of gold. Gold had been discovered in California in 1848. Thousands of people hoped to become wealthy.

Wagon trains formed single-file lines as they journeyed West.

The Hesters did not head to California Territory in search of wealth. They had money and lived comfortably. Sallie's father, Craven, was a successful lawyer. But Sallie's mother, Martha, was ill. Craven hoped that Martha's health would improve in the warm California climate.

The Hesters said good-bye to their friends and family in Indiana and began the adventure of a lifetime. They joined 48 other wagons to form a wagon train.

The Hesters' wagon train traveled 2,000 miles (3,219 kilometers) along the Oregon-California Trail. The wagon train members endured many hardships, including difficult weather and illness. Not all members survived the trip.

Sallie wrote about her experiences on the trail. Her diary describes what life was like for the thousands of pioneers who journeyed west in search of a better life.

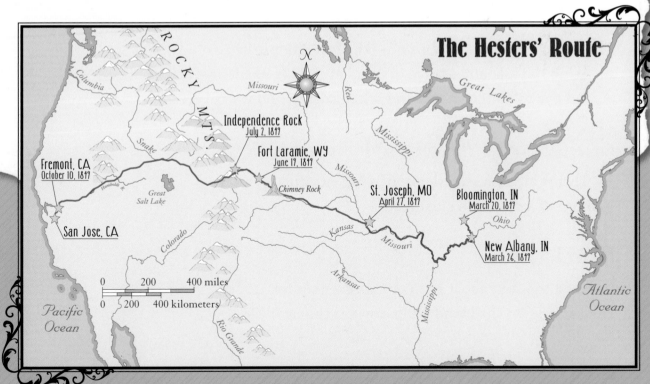

The Hesters' Route

Columbia

ROCKY MTS.

Missouri

Red

Great Lakes

Snake

Independence Rock
July 2, 1849

Mississippi

Fort Laramie, WY
June 19, 1849

Missouri

Fremont, CA
October 10, 1849

Humboldt R.

Great Salt Lake

Chimney Rock

St. Joseph, MO
April 27, 1849

Bloomington, IN
March 20, 1849

Ohio

San Jose, CA

Colorado

Kansas

Missouri

New Albany, IN
March 26, 1849

0   200   400 miles

0   200   400 kilometers

Arkansas

Mississippi

Atlantic Ocean

Pacific Ocean

Rio Grande

THE Diary OF Sallie Hester
1849–1850

Bloomington, Indiana, March 20, 1849 –

Our family, consisting of father, mother, two brothers and one sister, left this morning for that far and much talked of country, California. My father started our wagons one month in advance, to St. Joseph, Missouri, our starting point. We take the steamboat at New Albany [Indiana], going by water to St. Joe ... Our train numbered fifty wagons. The last hours were spent in bidding good bye to old friends. My mother is heartbroken over this separation of relatives and friends. Giving up old associations for what? Good health, perhaps ... The last good bye has been said—the last glimpse of our old home on the hill, and a wave of hand at the old Academy with a good bye to kind teachers and schoolmates, and we are off ...

New Albany, March 24 –

This is my first experience of a big city and my first glimpse of a river and steamboats.

March 26 –

Took the steamboat Meteor this evening for St. Joe. Now sailing on the broad Ohio, toward the far West.

April 3 –

On the Missouri River, the worst in the world, sticking on **sand bars** [sandbars] most of the time.

April 14 –

Our boat struck another sand bar and was obliged to land passengers ten miles [16 km] below St. Joe. Having our carriage with us, we were more fortunate than others ...

Sallie's diary entries appear word for word as they were written, whenever possible. Because the diary appears in its original form, you will notice misspellings and mistakes in grammar. To make Sallie's meaning clear, in some instances, corrections or explanations within a set of brackets sometimes follow the mistakes.

By the late 1800s, steamboats were a common sight on U.S. rivers, such as the Ohio.

sandbar–a ridge of sand in a river or bay

St. Joe, [Missouri,] April 27 —

Here we are at last, safe and sound. We expect to remain here several days, laying in supplies for the trip and waiting our turn to be **ferried** across the river. As far as the eye can reach, so great is the **emigration**, you see nothing but wagons. This <u>town</u> [St. Joseph] presents a striking appearance—a vast army on wheels—crowds of men, women, and lots of children and last but not least the cattle and horses upon which our lives depend.

St. Joseph was called a jumping-off town. Many Oregon-California Trail pioneers unloaded their wagons from steamships in jumping-off towns. They then started off on the trail. These towns were a place for pioneers to gather any last-minute supplies.

The Missouri River is the longest river in the United States. It forms the border between several states.

ferry—to travel in a ferry, which is a boat that regularly carries people across a stretch of water

Wagon Train Supplies

Pioneers had to be prepared for whatever they faced on the trail. Packing enough supplies was a key part of preparation. Here are just a few items wagon trains had:

WATER: Pioneers attached water barrels to the sides of their wagons. The water was used for drinking and cooking.

TOOLS AND WAGON PARTS: Pioneers brought tools to make repairs to their wagons and equipment. These tools included hammers and saws. Pioneers also carried supplies such as ropes, brake chains, and extra wagon axles and **tongues**.

FOOD: Hundreds of pounds of dried goods and meats were packed into wagons. Many pioneers tied a cow behind their wagons to provide fresh milk. Some people attached chicken coops to the sides of their wagons.

WEAPONS: Pioneers packed guns and other weapons for hunting and protection.

emigration—the leaving of one's own home country or region to live in another

tongue—a long wooden pole in front of a wagon that connects the wagon to the animals pulling it

9

May 21 —

Camped on the beautiful Blue River, 215 miles [346 km] from St. Joe, with plenty of wood and water and good grazing for our cattle. Our family all in good health. When we left St. Joe my mother had to be lifted in and out of our wagons; now she walks a mile or two without stopping, and gets in and out of the wagons as **spry** as a young girl. She is perfectly well. We had two deaths in our train within the past week of cholera—young men going West to seek their fortunes. We buried them on the banks of the Blue River, far from home and friends. This is a beautiful spot. The **Plains** are covered with flowers. We are in the Pawnee Nation, a dangerous and hostile tribe. We are obliged to watch them closely and double our guards at night. They never make their appearance during the day, but **skulk** around at night, steal cattle and do all the mischief they can.

In the mid-1800s, more than 2,000 Pawnee families lived in what are now Nebraska and Wyoming. Many wagon-train travelers feared the Pawnee because they were known as fierce warriors. But the Pawnee were one of the most helpful tribes to pioneers. They helped the United States stop other American Indians from attacking settlers.

When we camp at night, we form a corral with our wagons and pitch our tents on the outside, and inside of this corral we drive our cattle, with guards stationed on the outside of tents. We have a cooking stove made of sheet iron, a portable table, tin plates and cups, cheap knives and forks (best ones packed away), camp stools, etc. We sleep in our wagons on feather beds; the men who drive for us [sleep] in the tent ...

Pawnee Indians ride horses at one of their Nebraska camps in 1866.

spry—quick and light in motion
plain—a large, flat area of land with few trees
skulk—to move in a sneaky way

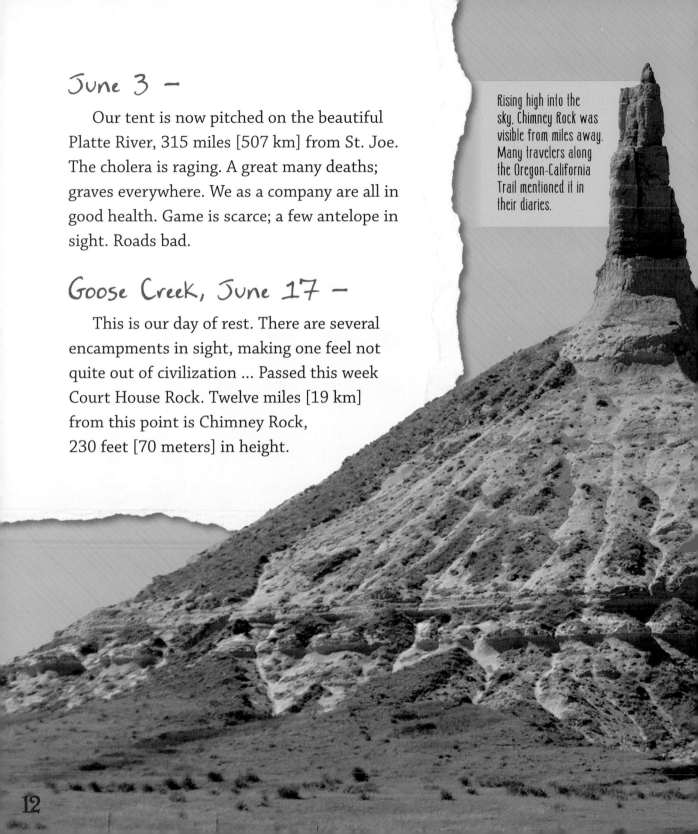

June 3 –

Our tent is now pitched on the beautiful Platte River, 315 miles [507 km] from St. Joe. The cholera is raging. A great many deaths; graves everywhere. We as a company are all in good health. Game is scarce; a few antelope in sight. Roads bad.

Goose Creek, June 17 –

This is our day of rest. There are several encampments in sight, making one feel not quite out of civilization ... Passed this week Court House Rock. Twelve miles [19 km] from this point is Chimney Rock, 230 feet [70 meters] in height.

Rising high into the sky, Chimney Rock was visible from miles away. Many travelers along the Oregon-California Trail mentioned it in their diaries.

Cholera

Cholera was one of the biggest dangers travelers faced on the Oregon-California Trail. Some pioneers who drank dirty water became sick with this deadly disease. People bathed and washed their livestock in rivers and streams. This dirty water often was the only drinking water available to the pioneers.

Once infected, victims suffered from diarrhea and vomiting, which led to dehydration. Cholera victims often died within hours of catching the disease. More than 1,500 pioneers died of cholera in 1849 alone. The disease continues to affect people in southern Asia, Latin America, and other parts of the world today.

Fort Laramie, [Wyoming,]
June 19 –

This fort is of **adobe**, enclosed with a high wall of the same. The entrance is a hole in the wall just large enough for a person to crawl through. The impression you have on entering is that you are in a small town. Men were engaged in all kinds of business from **blacksmith** up ...

Fort Laramie was built as a fur trading post in 1834. When Sallie traveled on the trail, the fort was very small. The adobe wall Sallie mentions was built to protect fort property. The wall was torn down as the fort grew in size.

June 21 –

Left camp and started over the Black Hills, sixty miles [97 km] over the worst road in the world. Have again struck the Platte and followed it until we came to the ferry. Here we had a great deal of trouble swimming our cattle across, taking our wagons to pieces, unloading and replacing our traps. A number of accidents happened here. A lady and four children were drowned through the carelessness of those in charge of the ferry.

The Black Hills are a low mountain range in present-day southwestern South Dakota and eastern Wyoming.

adobe—bricks made of mud and straw, dried and hardened by the heat of the sun

blacksmith—a person who makes and fixes objects made of iron

Eventually almost all travelers on the Oregon-California Trail had to cross the North Platte River. The first ferry on this river was available in 1847.

Dangerous River Crossings

Crossing rivers was a dangerous task for pioneers on the Oregon-California Trail. Rivers were often too deep to wade animals to the other side. In these cases pioneers often took the wheels off the wagons and floated them across. They then forced the oxen and other animals to swim across.

People drowned by falling from the wagons. Ferries operated on some large rivers, such as the Platte. However, the operators often overloaded the ferries. These heavy ferries were at risk of sinking. The Kansas, Snake, North Platte, and Green Rivers were some of the most difficult to cross.

July 2 —

Passed Independence Rock. This rock is covered with names. With great difficulty I found a place to cut mine. Twelve miles [19 km] from this is Devil's Gate. It's an opening in the mountain through which the Sweetwater River flows. Several of us climbed this mountain ... We made our way to the very edge of the cliff and looked down. We could hear the water dashing, splashing and roaring as if angry at the small space through which it was forced to pass. We were gone so long that the train was stopped and men were sent out in search of us ... During the week we passed the South Pass and the **summit** of the Rocky Mountains. Four miles from here are the Pacific Springs.

Independence Rock

Wagon trains began their journey along the Oregon-California Trail in early spring. Beginning the trip at this time was important. Pioneers had to reach the west coast before winter. If they did not, they were likely to experience dangerous snowstorms crossing the Rocky Mountains.

Most wagon trains tried to reach the landmark known as Independence Rock by July 1. The giant turtle-shaped mound is 700 feet (213 m) wide. Fur trappers who celebrated Independence Day there in the early 1800s named the rock in honor of the holiday.

Thousands of pioneers carved their names on Independence Rock. Today visitors to the famous landmark in Wyoming can read many of the names.

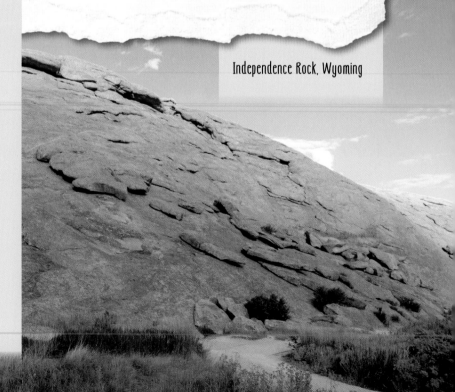

Independence Rock, Wyoming

July 4 –

... At this point saw lots of dead cattle left by the emigrants to starve and die. Took a cutoff; had neither wood nor water for fifty-two miles [84 km]. Traveled in the night. Arrived at Green River next day at two o' clock in the afternoon. Lay by two days to rest man and beast after our long and weary journey.

The South Pass was a passage through the Rocky Mountains. It marked the boundary between unorganized territory and the U.S-owned Oregon Territory.

The death of oxen and cattle was a serious problem for those on the Oregon-California Trail.

summit—the highest point of a mountain

July 29 –

Passed Soda **Springs** [Idaho]. Two miles [3 km] further on are the Steamboat Springs. They puff and blow and throw the water high in the air ...

August 3 –

Took another cut-off this week called Sublets [Sublette Cutoff] Struck Raft River; from thence to Swamp Creek. Passed some beautiful scenery, high cliffs of rocks resembling old ruins or dilapidated buildings.

Hot Springs, August 18 –

Camped on a branch of Mary's River, a very disagreeable and unpleasant place on account of the water being so hot ... Roads are rocky and trying to our wagons, and the dust is horrible. The men wear veils tied over their hats as a protection. When we reach camp at night they are covered with dust from head to heels.

Steamboat Springs were located in present-day Idaho. When Sallie traveled on the Oregon-California Trail, the water shot high into the air. The springs made loud chugging noises that were similar to the sound of a steamboat engine. Today the springs are flooded. Present-day visitors can no longer see the amazing sights early pioneers did.

Sublette Cutoff was a shortcut on the Oregon-California Trail that saved about 3 days of travel time. The cutoff is still visible today.

Humboldt River [Nevada], August 20 –

We are now 348 miles [560 km] from the mines. We expect to travel that distance in three weeks and a half. Water and grass scarce.

St. Mary's River, August 25 –

Still traveling down the Humboldt. Grass has been scarce until today. Though the water is not fit to drink—**slough** water—we are obliged to use it, for it's all we have.

spring—a place where water rises up from underground

slough—a ditch filled with deep mud

St. Mary's, September 2 —

After coming through a dreary region of country for two or three days, we arrived Saturday night. We had good grass but the water was bad. Remained over Sunday. Had preaching in camp.

September 4 —

Left the place [St. Mary's] where we camped last Sunday. Traveled six miles [10 km]. Stopped and cut grass for the cattle and supplied ourselves with water for the desert. Had a trying time crossing. Several of our cattle gave out and we left one. Our journey through the desert was from Monday, three o'clock in the afternoon, until Thursday morning at sunrise, September 6.

St. Mary's camp was one of the last major camps pioneers came upon before reaching California.

The desert in present-day Nevada that Sallie crossed is called the 40 Mile Desert. It was one of the most dreaded and dangerous parts of the Oregon-California Trail. Pioneers traveled it by night because daytime temperatures were too high.

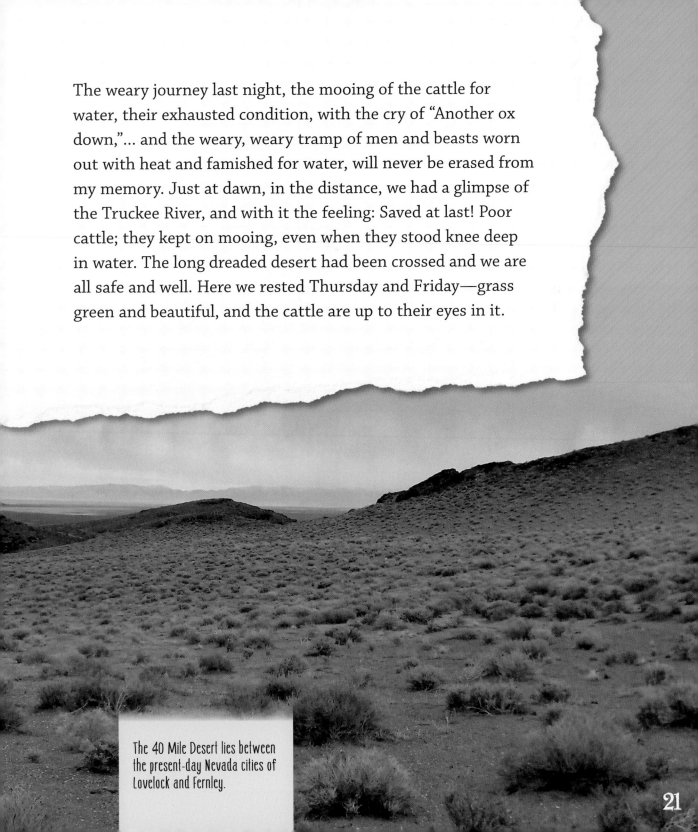

The weary journey last night, the mooing of the cattle for water, their exhausted condition, with the cry of "Another ox down,"... and the weary, weary tramp of men and beasts worn out with heat and famished for water, will never be erased from my memory. Just at dawn, in the distance, we had a glimpse of the Truckee River, and with it the feeling: Saved at last! Poor cattle; they kept on mooing, even when they stood knee deep in water. The long dreaded desert had been crossed and we are all safe and well. Here we rested Thursday and Friday—grass green and beautiful, and the cattle are up to their eyes in it.

The 40 Mile Desert lies between the present-day Nevada cities of Lovelock and Fernley.

September 8 –

Traveled fourteen miles [23 km]; crossed Truckee twelve times.

September 11 –

Made eighteen miles [29 km]. Crossed Truckee River ten times. Came near being drowned at one of the crossings. Got frightened and jumped out of the carriage into the water. The current was very swift and carried me some distance down the stream.

Truckee River, Nevada

September 14 —

... We crossed the summit of the Sierra Nevada. It was night when we reached the top, and I shall never forget our descent to the place where we are now encamped—our tedious march with pine knots blazing in the darkness and the tall, majestic pines towering above our heads. The scene was grand and gloomy beyond description. We could not ride—roads too narrow and rocky—so we trudged along, keeping pace with the wagons as best we could. This is another picture engraven upon the tablets of memory. It was a footsore and weary crowd that reached that night our present camping place.

The Sierra Nevada mountain range lies in present-day eastern California. It is more than 400 miles (644 km) long. The highest peaks rise more than 14,000 feet (4,267 meters).

September 17 –

Left camp this morning. Traveled down to the lower end of the valley. Lay by two days. Had preaching out under the pines at night. The men built a fire and we all gathered around it in camp-meeting style.

September 19 –

Started once more. Roads bad, almost impassable. After traveling for twenty-five miles [40 km] we halted for one day. Good grass three miles [5 km] from camp.

September 21 –

Reached Bear Valley by descending a tremendous hill. We let the wagons down with ropes. Stopped over Sunday. At Sleepy Hollow we again let our wagons down the mountain with ropes ... Cut down trees for our cattle to browse on. Thanks to a kind Providence we are nearing the end of our long and perilous journey. Came on to Grass Valley and rested four or five days.

Vernon, California [near San Francisco], October 6 –

Well, after a five month's trip from St. Joe, Missouri, our party of fifty wagons, now only thirteen, has at last reached this haven of rest. Strangers in a strange land—what will our future be? ...

The hill in the Sierra Nevada Mountains that Sallie mentions was very dangerous. Pioneers had to lower their wagons down 5,200 feet (1,585 m). The steep descent was made after crossing a narrow mountain opening. This opening is now called Emigrant Gap.

Fremont, [California,] October 10 –

This is a small town on the opposite side of the river from Vernon. My father has decided to remain here for the winter, as the rains have set in and we are worn out. We have had a small house put up of two rooms made of boards with **puncheon** floor. On this mother has a carpet which she brought with us and we feel quite fine, as our neighbors have the ground for a floor.

The rooms are lined with heavy blue cloth. Our beds are put up in bunk style on one side of the room and curtained off. Back of these rooms we have pitched our tent, which answers as a store room, and the back of the lot is enclosed with a brush fence. My father has gone to Sacramento to lay in provisions for the winter.

The steep cliffs of the Sierra Nevada were one of the last big challenges before reaching California.

puncheon—a split log or heavy slab with the face smoothed

25

Christmas, 1849 –

Still raining. This has been a sad Christmas for mother. She is homesick, longs for her old home and friends ... Was invited to a **candy pull** and had a nice time. Rather a number of young folks camped here. This is a funny looking town anyway. Most of the houses are built of brush. Now that the rains have set in, people are beginning to think of something more substantial. Some have log cabins, others have **clapboards** like ours.

January 12 [1850] –

Water over the banks of the river, all over town except in a few places. Our house has escaped, though it's all around us. Mother has planted a garden in the rear of [the] lot and that has been swept away. Nearly everybody is up to their knees in mud and water. Some have boots. As far as the eye can reach you see nothing but water. It's horrible. Wish I was back in Indiana. Snakes are plenty. They come down the river, crawl under our bed and everywhere.

April 1 –

Quite a number of our old friends who crossed the Plains with us have stopped here for the winter, which makes it pleasant for mother. My father has gone to San Jose ... to look for a permanent home.

Forests in the West provided pioneers with plenty of wood. Small wooden houses were common.

April 27 –

My father has returned from San Jose. He gives glowing accounts of the place and lovely climate. We have not seen very much as yet of the mild and delightful climate of California so much talked about. We leave next month for San Jose. We are all glad that we are going to have a home somewhere at last.

candy pull—a party at which taffy or molasses candy is made

clapboard—a narrow board usually thicker at one edge than the other

Honoring a Part of U.S. History

Sallie Hester's family and other members of their wagon train were just a few of the more than 350,000 people who traveled west. All of these pioneers were part of the U.S. movement known as Westward Expansion.

The Oregon-California Trail that Sallie traveled on was one of the main routes west. The trip was difficult and life-threatening. Historians estimate that more than 20,000 people died on the journey. Today people remember the hardships that the brave pioneers faced on their westward journeys.

Timeline

- Dates in Sallie Hester's life
- Important dates in Westward Expansion

1848

Mexico agrees to give the United States California Territory and other land that became present-day states, including Arizona and New Mexico.

James Marshall discovers gold in California's American River. His discovery leads to the California Gold Rush (1847-1859).

1843

Wagon trains begin to travel the Oregon Trail.

1835

Sallie is born.

1835 ⟵ **1845**

1849-March 20

The Hester family leaves Bloomington, Indiana, to begin their journey along the Oregon-California trail.

1849-July 2

The Hesters' wagon train passes Independence Rock in Wyoming.

1850

The Hesters leave for San Jose.

1849-September

The Hesters reach California.

1850

California becomes a U.S. state.

1850

Glossary

adobe (uh-DOH-bee)—bricks made of mud and straw, dried and hardened by the heat of the sun

blacksmith (BLAK-smith)—a person who makes and fixes things made of iron

candy pull (KAN-dee PUL)—a party at which taffy or molasses candy is made

clapboard (KLAP-bord)—a narrow board usually thicker at one edge than the other

dilapidated (duh-LAP-uh-day-ted)—in need of repair

emigration (e-muh-GRAY-shuhn)—the leaving of one's own home country or region to live in another

ferry (FAYR-ee)—a boat that regularly carries people across a stretch of water

plain (PLANE)—a large, flat area of land with few trees

puncheon (PUN-chun)—a split log or heavy slab with the face smoothed

sandbar (SAND-bar)—a ridge of sand in a river or bay

skulk (SKULK)—to move in a sneaky way

slough (SLOO)—a ditch filled with deep mud

spring (SPRING)—a place where water rises up from underground

spry (SPRY)—quick and light in motion

summit (SUHM-it)—the highest point of a mountain

tongue (TUHNG)—the long wooden pole in front of a wagon that connected the wagon to the animals pulling it

Read More

Doeden, Matt. *The Oregon Trail: An Interactive History Adventure.* You Choose: History. North Mankato, Minn.: Capstone Press, 2014.

Friedman, Mel. *The Oregon Trail.* A True Book. New York: Children's Press, 2010.

Critical Thinking Using the Common Core

1. Sallie describes the Pawnee Indians as "dangerous" and "hostile." However, the explanation box on page 10 describes the tribe as helpful. What do you think accounts for the differences in these narratives? (Integration of Knowledge and Ideas)

2. Look at the timeline and text on pages 28 and 29. Wagon trains began using the Oregon Trail in 1843 and California became a state in 1850. Population growth is one factor that helped lead to statehood in the 1800s. Discuss what you think might have been the positive and negative effects of such a sudden surge in California's population, using information from the text and from online sources. (Craft and Structure)

3. On page 24, Sallie says that her wagon party started with 50 wagons, but now is only 13. What does this tell you about the trip's difficulty? Look at online and print resources about similar journeys to find out what happened to those who did not make it to their destinations. Compare and contrast these journeys. (Integration of Knowledge and Ideas)

Internet Sites

FactHound offers a safe, fun way to find Internet sites related to this book. All of the sites on FactHound have been researched by our staff.

Here's all you do:

Visit *www.facthound.com*

Type in this code: 9781476541938

 Check out projects, games and lots more at
www.capstonekids.com

Index